SRA
MULTIPLE SKILLS
SERIES: Reading

Third Edition

Richard A. Boning

SRA McGraw-Hill

Columbus, Ohio

*A Division of The **McGraw·Hill** Companies*

SRA/McGraw-Hill

A Division of The **McGraw·Hill** *Companies*

Send all inquiries to:
SRA/McGraw-Hill
8787 Orion Place
Columbus, OH 43240-4027

ISBN 0-02-688444-5

6 7 8 9   BSE   07 06 05 04 03

PURPOSE

The *Multiple Skills Series* is a nonconsumable reading program designed to develop a cluster of key reading skills and to integrate these skills with each other and with the other language arts. *Multiple Skills* is also diagnostic, making it possible for you to identify specific types of reading skills that might be causing difficulty for individual students.

FOR WHOM

The twelve levels of the *Multiple Skills Series* are geared to students who comprehend on the pre-first- through ninth-grade reading levels.

- The Picture Level is for children who have not acquired a basic sight vocabulary.
- The Preparatory 1 Level is for children who have developed a limited basic sight vocabulary.
- The Preparatory 2 Level is for children who have a basic sight vocabulary but are not yet reading on the first-grade level.
- Books A through I are appropriate for students who can read on grade levels one through nine respectively. Because of their high interest level, the books may also be used effectively with students functioning at these levels of competence in other grades.

The **Multiple Skills Series Placement Tests** will help you determine the appropriate level for each student.

PLACEMENT TESTS

The Elementary Placement Test (for grades Pre-1 through 3) and the Midway Placement Tests (for grades 4–9) will help you place each student properly. The tests consist of representative units selected from the series. The test books contain two forms, X and Y. One form may be used for placement and the second as a post-test to measure progress. The tests are easy to administer and score. Blackline Masters are provided for worksheets and student performance profiles.

THE BOOKS

This third edition of the *Multiple Skills Series* maintains the quality and focus that have distinguished this program for over 25 years. The series includes four books at each level, Picture Level through Level I. Each book in the Picture Level through Level B contains 25 units. Each book in Level C through Level I contains 50 units. The units within each book increase in difficulty. The books within a level also increase in difficulty—Level A, Book 2 is slightly more difficult than Level A, Book 1, and so on. This gradual increase in difficulty permits students to advance from one book to the next and from one level to the next without frustration.

Each book contains an **About This Book** page, which explains the skills to the students and shows them how to approach reading the selections and questions. In the lowest levels, you should read About This Book to the children.

The questions that follow each unit are designed to develop specific reading skills. In the lowest levels, you should read the questions to the children.

In Level D, the question pattern in each unit is
1. Title (main idea)
2. Stated detail
3. Stated detail
4. Inference or conclusion
5. Vocabulary

The **Language Activity Pages** (LAP) in each level consist of four parts: Exercising Your Skill, Expanding Your Skill, Exploring Language, and Expressing Yourself. These pages lead the students beyond the book through a broadening spiral of writing, speaking, and other individual and group language activities that apply, extend, and integrate the skills being developed. You may use all, some, or none of the activities in any LAP; however, some LAP activities depend on preceding ones. In the lowest levels, you should read the LAPs to the children.

In Levels C-I, each set of Language Activity Pages focuses on a particular skill developed through the book. Emphasis progresses from the most concrete to the most abstract:

First LAP	Details
Second LAP	Vocabulary
Third LAP	Main ideas
Last LAP	Inferences and conclusions

SESSIONS

The *Multiple Skills Series* is basically an individualized reading program that may be used with small groups or an entire class. Short sessions are the most effective. Use a short session every day or every other day, completing a few units in each session. Time allocated to the Language Activity Pages depends on the abilities of the individual students.

SCORING

Students should record their answers on the reproducible worksheets. The worksheets make scoring easier and provide uniform records of the children's work. Using worksheets also avoids consuming the books.

Because it is important for the students to know how they are progressing, you should score the units as soon as they've been completed. Then you can discuss the questions and activities with the students and encourage them to justify their responses. Many of the LAPs are open-ended and do not lend themselves to an objective score; for this reason, there are no answer keys for these pages.

A careful reader thinks about the writer's words and pays attention to what the story or article is mainly about. A careful reader also "reads between the lines" because a writer does not tell the reader everything. A careful reader tries to figure out the meaning of new words too. As you read the stories and articles in this book, you will practice all of these reading skills.

First you will read a story and choose a good title for it. The title will tell something about the **main idea** of the article or story. To choose a good title, you must know what the story or article is mainly about.

The next two questions will ask you about facts that are stated in the story or article. To answer these questions, read carefully. Pay attention to the **details.**

The fourth question will ask you to figure out **something the writer doesn't tell you directly.** For example, you might read that Dr. Fujihara received an emergency call, drove to Elm Street, and rushed into a house. Even though the writer doesn't tell you directly, you can figure out that Dr. Fujihara knows how to drive and that someone in the house is probably sick. You use the information the author provides plus your own knowledge and experience to figure out what is probably true.

The last question will ask you to tell the meaning of a word in the story or article. You can figure out what the word means by studying its **context**—the other words and sentences in the story. Read the following sentences.

The house was surrounded by trees. They helped keep the house cool in summer. Unfortunately, they also cut out most of the light. A giant *hemlock* just outside Marcia's window made her room dark and gloomy.

Did you figure out that a hemlock is a kind of tree? What clues in the story helped you figure this out?

This book will help you practice your reading skills. As you learn to use all of these skills together, you will become a better reader.

Almost everyone who lives where there is ice or snow has made a snow fort or house at one time or another. In 1896, there was no house made of ice that was *equal* to the Ice Palace in Leadville, Colorado.

Can you picture a building made almost entirely of ice and as big as ten football fields? The Ice Palace in Leadville, Colorado, was that big. It cost $60,000 to build and had walls eight feet thick! Inside were a large skating rink, a restaurant, and two huge dance halls.

Thousands of people came to see the Ice Palace—but not for long. In ten weeks the ice melted, and the Ice Palace was out of business.

---

1. The best title is—
   (A) Building Forts of Snow and Ice
   (B) The Thickest Walls Ever Built
   (C) How to Destroy a Building
   (D) An Amazing Ice Palace

2. The Ice Palace in Leadville had—
   (A) a racetrack   (B) a horse show
   (C) two dance halls   (D) a baseball field

3. The Ice Palace was open—
   (A) 18 years   (B) eight months
   (C) three weeks   (D) ten weeks

4. The Ice Palace may have stayed in business longer if—
   (A) more people had come   (B) the weather had been warmer
   (C) the walls were thinner   (D) the weather had been colder

5. The word "equal" in line three means—
   (A) be smaller than   (B) look as warm as
   (C) be the same as   (D) weigh as little as

The squirrel has a long tail for its short body. The squirrel is very happy it does have such a long tail, because it uses that tail for many different purposes.

When the sun gets hot, the squirrel holds its tail above its head like an umbrella. In the cold, the squirrel uses the tail as a warm blanket. Some squirrels even use their tails to fight with. The most important use for the squirrel's tail is for balance. With its tail for balancing, the squirrel can speed from branch to branch at over seventeen miles per hour.

No wonder the squirrel is so *content* with its long tail!

1. The best title is—
   (A) Tall Trees
   (B) How Squirrels Use Their Tails
   (C) An Interesting Animal
   (D) Learning to Fight with Tails

2. When it is hot, the squirrel uses its tail as—
   (A) a blanket   (B) an umbrella
   (C) a broom   (D) a club

3. The most important use of a squirrel's tail is for—
   (A) washing   (B) swimming
   (C) balance   (D) warmth

4. The story suggests that a squirrel spends part of its time—
   (A) in school   (B) in water
   (C) chasing cars   (D) in trees

5. The word "content" in line ten means—
   (A) sad   (B) happy
   (C) clumsy   (D) little

In 1853, Levi Strauss went to San Francisco to sell *dry goods*. On the way there, his shipmates bought everything he had brought with him except for one roll of heavy brown canvas. Strauss planned to sell it to someone who wanted to make a tent or a cover for a wagon.

The gold miners Strauss met were not interested in buying canvas. They wanted sturdy pants that could hold up to hard work. Strauss thought about what the miners said and used the canvas to make pants. Everyone who saw them wanted "those pants of Levi's." Strauss was in business.

Strauss replaced the brown canvas with blue denim and made a few small changes to the pants, but the basic style is the same today as it was 100 years ago. If you own a pair of Levi's, you own a piece of history.

---

1. The best title is—
    (A) Gold Miner's Clothing
    (B) Welcome to California
    (C) I Need Pants
    (D) The Story of Levi's

2. The first people to wear Levi's were—
    (A) shipmates   (B) history teachers
    (C) gold miners   (D) tent makers

3. Levi's were originally made out of—
    (A) blue denim   (B) brown canvas
    (C) blue canvas   (D) pink linen

4. You can tell that Strauss was a good—
    (A) swimmer   (B) gold miner
    (C) businessman   (D) painter

5. The words "dry goods" in line one mean—
    (A) scissors   (B) lumber
    (C) gold   (D) fabric

Dogs can be used for a variety of lifesaving jobs. Some dogs are specially trained to track and rescue people who are lost in the wilderness. Other dogs seem to have a natural ability to sense danger and take action without any training at all.

In 1996, ten-year-old Josh Carlisle was reported missing from his home. Volunteers began to search the mountains nearby. Nighttime temperatures dropped below freezing, and Josh was lost.

On the third day, searchers heard a dog barking and followed the sound. They found Josh snuggled up with a dachshund and a mutt. The *stray* dogs had stayed with Josh. They played with him, kept him warm, and helped him find water. They made sure Josh got home safe and sound, and they haven't left his side since.

---

1. The best title is—
   (A) How to Survive at Night
   (B) Josh's Best Friends
   (C) How to Train a Dog
   (D) Life in the Mountains

2. Dogs can be specially trained to—
   (A) save lives   (B) sense danger
   (C) find a home   (D) stay warm

3. At night, the temperature was—
   (A) warm   (B) below zero
   (C) below freezing   (D) ten degrees

4. The story suggests that Josh's family must have—
   (A) hated the dogs   (B) sold the dogs
   (C) washed the dogs   (D) adopted the dogs

5. The word "stray" in line ten means—
   (A) fuzzy   (B) homeless
   (C) skinny   (D) housebroken

UNIT 5

A sport that many people enjoy is riding the waves on a surfboard. It takes good balance to do it well. That is why in 1961, in California, surfboard riders put skate wheels on pieces of wood. They wanted to practice balancing when they couldn't be *surfing* on the ocean.

In 1963, a company had a wonderful idea—to make boards with skate wheels for people who didn't even surf. The boards became popular and are known as skateboards.

Boys and girls all around the country enjoy using skateboards. However, since skateboarding is done on cement, children know that they must protect themselves. Knee and elbow pads are often used to make the sport safer and still allow for lots of fun.

---

1. The best title is—
   - (A) How Skateboards Began
   - (B) Riding Waves in California
   - (C) How to Make a Surfboard
   - (D) Enjoying the Ocean

2. The story says that skateboards are used on—
   - (A) water
   - (B) ice
   - (C) cement
   - (D) grass

3. Skateboards began in—
   - (A) 1951
   - (B) California
   - (C) New Mexico
   - (D) 1971

4. The story suggests that skateboards—
   - (A) are silly
   - (B) are no fun
   - (C) can be dangerous
   - (D) are not popular

5. The word "surfing" in line four means—
   - (A) riding
   - (B) sinking
   - (C) looking
   - (D) walking

You have probably heard of the *Mayflower*. The *Mayflower* was the ship that carried the Pilgrims from England to America. If you saw the *Mayflower* today, you would never recognize it. It is a barn!

After the *Mayflower* brought the Pilgrims to America, it was still used for a few years. Often it carried rice and other food between England and America. Later, however, it became too *timeworn* to sail. It returned to England to stay.

There, someone took the ship apart and used the wood to make a barn. The barn still stands today in Buckingham.

1. The best title is—
   (A) The Barns of England
   (B) The Pilgrims Come to America
   (C) The *Mayflower*—Still Sailing
   (D) A Ship That Became a Barn

2. The story says that the *Mayflower* once carried—
   (A) tea   (B) potatoes
   (C) rice   (D) tobacco

3. Today the *Mayflower* is—
   (A) still sailing   (B) a museum
   (C) being repaired   (D) a barn

4. We can tell from the story that Buckingham is in—
   (A) America   (B) England
   (C) the ocean   (D) Canada

5. The word "timeworn" in line six means—
   (A) new   (B) fast
   (C) old   (D) beautiful

For a few years, they were one of the top bands in the whole world. They were Menudo, the five "little guys" from Puerto Rico. When they went to New York in 1983, ten thousand screaming fans met them at the airport. In Mexico City they performed for 100,000 people. One store in Venezuela sold $3 million worth of Menudo T-shirts and records in a single week.

Then the band all but disappeared. Maybe it was the *constant* changing of band members. When a member of the group turned sixteen, he had to leave. That was the rule. When it happened to Robby Rosa, the fans' favorite, people seemed to grow tired of Menudo. Some fans are sad, though. Menudo, says one fan, "made you feel good."

1. The best title is—
   (A) Rock Music in 1983
   (B) A Band Called Menudo
   (C) Robby Rosa's Career
   (D) Making Money Through Music

2. Menudo started in—
   (A) New York   (B) Puerto Rico
   (C) Mexico   (D) Venezuela

3. When a band member became sixteen, he—
   (A) sang better   (B) grew tired
   (C) got more money   (D) had to leave

4. Fans of Menudo—
   (A) were all young boys   (B) grew too old
   (C) made the rules   (D) wanted Robby Rosa to stay

5. The word "constant" in line seven means—
   (A) wonderful   (B) popular
   (C) endless   (D) weekly

Michelle was floating on her back in the warm blue water, her eyes closed against the bright sun. Then she heard a splash. She opened her eyes and saw a gray fin poking out of the water, only a few feet away. Then she saw another fin. Sharks! Michelle had read about sharks attacking swimmers. She tried to stay still. The sharks were circling, and they were getting closer!

Then suddenly the sharks disappeared. Michelle jumped when she felt something press against her side. But it was not a shark. It was a dolphin! With its nose, the dolphin nudged Michelle toward shore. It swam beside her until she was safe. Michelle *vowed* never to swim alone again.

1. The best title is—
   (A) Killer Sharks
   (B) The Dolphin Trainer
   (C) Saved by a Dolphin
   (D) Warm water Fish

2. Michelle knew that sharks could—
   (A) be friendly   (B) not swim well
   (C) attack   (D) not escape

3. When the dolphin appeared, the sharks—
   (A) disappeared   (B) attacked
   (C) jumped   (D) circled

4. You can tell that dolphins can—
   (A) be dangerous   (B) be friendly
   (C) help sharks   (D) kill sharks

5. The word "vowed" in line ten means—
   (A) demanded   (B) feared
   (C) promised   (D) trained

An angler is a person who fishes with a hook and line. An angler fish is a fish that does its own fishing. This strange-looking sea creature has its own "fishing rod," which grows out of the top of its head and hangs in front of its mouth. The "rod" has a shiny end. Other fish are *attracted* to it, thinking it is something good to eat. When a fish swims close enough—zap!—the angler fish snaps up another meal!

The female angler fish grows to about three feet in length, but the male is only three inches long. The male does not have a fishing rod, so the female does the fishing for them both.

1. The best title is—
   (A) Males and Females
   (B) A Fish That Fishes for Fish
   (C) Catching an Angler Fish
   (D) Fresh-water Fishing

2. The female sea angler grows to be—
   (A) three inches long   (B) as long as a fishing rod
   (C) three feet long   (D) the same size as the male

3. The angler fish's fishing rod—
   (A) is on its head   (B) is very long
   (C) is a fin   (D) has a hook

4. When other fish swim near the angler fish, they are—
   (A) fierce   (B) not aware of the danger
   (C) swimming quickly   (D) hard to catch

5. The word "attracted" in line five means—
   (A) caught   (B) warned
   (C) drawn   (D) eaten

Have you ever bought something and had to pay extra money called a "tax"? The money from taxes is used to run the government. We pay taxes when we buy cars, houses, and many other things. Long ago, people had to pay taxes on some very strange things.

In New York, anyone who wore a wig had to pay a tax. In Russia, there was a tax on beards. If the tax wasn't paid, the beard was *clipped* off. In Holland, people had to pay a tax for every window in their house, so people began building houses without windows.

Today there are still taxes, but at least most of them make more sense.

1. The best title is—
   (A) Growing Beards
   (B) Strange Taxes of Long Ago
   (C) Building Houses Without Windows
   (D) What It Costs to Buy a Car

2. In Russia, there was a tax on—
   (A) windows   (B) houses
   (C) cars   (D) beards

3. There was a tax on wigs in—
   (A) New York   (B) China
   (C) Germany   (D) England

4. The story suggests that paying taxes is—
   (A) new   (B) not new
   (C) not needed   (D) a game

5. The word "clipped" in line six means—
   (A) thrown   (B) turned
   (C) cut   (D) painted

For Tia Hunnicut, her dolls meant business. She didn't play with them. She made them! Tia started *constructing* dolls when she was 13. Tia's business, called Tia's Doll Emporium, started out in her mother's house in San Francisco. Tia designed all the dolls' clothing, painted their faces, and put the pieces together. Tia's business grew so large that she hired three people to help her.

In 1986 the mayor of San Francisco set aside a day for the city to honor Tia. A magazine named her the All-American Girl of the Year. "There are no limits to what you can do," said Tia, "if you believe in yourself and work very, very hard."

1. The best title is—
   (A) A San Francisco Magazine
   (B) Dolls Throughout History
   (C) Dolls Were Her Business
   (D) How to Make Dolls

2. Tia started making dolls when she was—
   (A) 12   (B) 13
   (C) 14   (D) 15

3. In 1986 Tia was honored by—
   (A) her family   (B) the president
   (C) the state of California (D) the city of San Francisco

4. Tia was—
   (A) unhappy   (B) clever and determined
   (C) the state of California (D) lazy

5. The word "constructing" in line two means—
   (A) making   (B) admiring
   (C) using   (D) improving

Have you ever gotten into trouble for clowning around in school? There is one school where teachers insist that students clown around! That school is Clown College in Florida, where students learn to be circus clowns.

Clown College is not as easy as you may think. Only about fifty students of the thousands who try out are chosen. They go to school from 8:30 in the morning until 10:00 at night for eight weeks. They learn how to ride a horse, tumble, walk a high wire, and run on stilts. They learn how to paint their faces, too. Each clown's face is different, for a clown never copies another clown's look.

If clowning around is something you can't *resist* doing, maybe you should think about Clown College.

---

1. The best title is—
   (A) Circus Clowns
   (B) Going to College in Florida
   (C) Circus Jobs
   (D) A College for Clowns

2. Clown College lasts—
   (A) ten weeks   (B) eight weeks
   (C) one year   (D) fifty weeks

3. The one thing every clown does differently is—
   (A) ride a horse   (B) run on stilts
   (C) paint a face   (D) tumble

4. The students in Clown College must be—
   (A) wealthy   (B) over twenty
   (C) good ball players   (D) serious

5. The word "resist" in line eleven means—
   (A) enjoy yourself   (B) give in to
   (C) stop yourself from   (D) think of

A. Exercising Your Skill

Facts are statements that can be proved true. For example, the statement "The female angler fish grows to about three feet in length" is a fact. You can prove the statement by looking in a good book that tells about angler fish.

Do you know any other facts about fish? See if you can list four facts before you read on.

Now read the paragraph below. After you have finished reading, list four facts about the remora fish that you learned from the paragraph.

The oceans contain many strange kinds of fish. One kind is the remora (say "rih MORE uh"), or "sucker" fish. The remora looks like an ordinary fish except for one thing. The top of its head is flat and has a kind of suction cup on it. The remora uses this suction cup to stick to other, bigger, fish. In this way the remora can get around without having to swim. What is more, it gets free meals. Each time the big fish catches its food, the remora lets go to eat whatever food is left behind. Then it attaches itself to the big fish once more. In some parts of the world people who fish use remoras as live bait for catching sea turtles or other fish. They tie a line around the remora's tail, then let it swim away. When the remora attaches itself to a fish or a turtle, the fisher hauls in the line with the remora attached. The remora is one fish that uses its head!

B. Expanding Your Skill

Compare your list of fish facts with those your classmates wrote. How many different fish facts did the class come up with? List them on the chalkboard.

C. Exploring Language

Choose one of these activities.

1. Find out more about one of the strange fish listed below. An encyclopedia is a good place to start. A book about sea life is another. Once you have chosen your strange fish, write a paragraph of five or six sentences about it. Use your own words. Give your paragraph a title.

> 1. catfish   2. grunion   3. flying fish   4. puffer fish
>
> 5. sea horse   6. mudskipper   7. cleaner wrasse

2. Use your own words to complete one of these paragraphs. Include as many facts as you can, and give your paragraph a title.

(Title)

The biggest fish I ever caught was _____

_____ . . . .

(Title)

Fish make excellent pets. _____

_____ . . .

(Title)

I like (or do not like) to eat fish. _____

_____ . . .

D. Expressing Yourself

Choose one of these activities.

1. If you fish, bring some of your gear to class. Explain how to use it in a talk to your classmates.
2. Invent your own strange fish. Write a paragraph that describes how the fish looks and what it does. Draw a picture of your imaginary fish.

Fingerprints are the pattern of fine lines on the tips of the fingers. Because everyone's fingerprints are different, they are a *foolproof* way to tell who a person is. Fingerprinting has long been used in police work. Now, new technology is making it useful to businesses, such as banks, that require positive identification.

Until recently, fingerprinting was done by rolling the fingertip over an ink pad and then pressing it onto a sheet of paper. It worked fine, but it was messy. Now fingerprinting can be done by pressing the fingertip against a glass plate. The image is scanned and then copied.

In the near future, people may not need to remember a special number, code, or password to open doors or access accounts. Their identification will be right at their fingertips.

---

1. The best title is—
   (A) Fingerprinting Then and Now
   (B) Police Work in the U.S.
   (C) Say Goodbye to Ink Pads
   (D) Who Are You?

2. A good way to identify a person is by—
   (A) asking the police   (B) making a fingerprint
   (C) asking for a password   (D) taking a picture

3. Before scanners were used, fingerprinting was done with—
   (A) a camera   (B) a copier
   (C) an ink pad   (D) a felt-tip pen

4. Using fingerprints helps make identification—
   (A) less perfect   (B) more exact
   (C) more difficult   (D) more common

5. The word "foolproof" in line two means—
   (A) foolish   (B) ancient
   (C) sure   (D) strange

There are many boat races throughout the world, but none is as strange as the one held each year at Alice Springs, Australia. Alice Springs is in the desert, and the river in which the boats race is almost always dry!

In this most unusual race, the boats have no bottoms. The crews run inside the boats as they hold them above the dried-up Todd River.

The boat race started in 1961. Now it's the biggest event of the year around Alice Springs. People come from hundreds of miles around to see the only dry boat race in the world. The only thing that could *ruin* the race is a very heavy rain!

---

1. The best title is—
   (A) An Unusual Boat Race
   (B) Boat Races Around the World
   (C) A Rain Storm
   (D) Building Boats

2. The boats in the race at Alice Springs have—
   (A) paddles   (B) oars
   (C) sails   (D) no bottoms

3. Alice Springs is in—
   (A) America   (B) a forest
   (C) a desert   (D) England

4. During the boat races in Alice Springs, no one has ever—
   (A) won   (B) watched
   (C) drowned   (D) lost

5. The word "ruin" in line ten means—
   (A) return   (B) meet
   (C) enter   (D) spoil

Georgia "Tiny" Broadwick made the first of her 1,100 parachute jumps in 1908, when she was fourteen years old. She became well known as an expert on parachutes.

The Army asked Broadwick to test a new kind of parachute. It was smaller and lighter than other parachutes of her day, but, like them, it was *secured* to the airplane with a rope that would open the chute. When Broadwick jumped, the rope caught on the tail of the airplane. Fortunately, she was able to shake it loose and float safely to the ground. Broadwick tried the jump again. This time she held the rope and opened the parachute herself. That was the world's first free-fall parachute jump.

---

1. The best title is—
   (A) Life in 1908
   (B) Parachute Jumping Today
   (C) Making New Kinds of Parachutes
   (D) Tiny Broadwick, Parachute Expert

2. Broadwick made her first jump when she was—
   (A) eleven years old   (B) fourteen years old
   (C) twenty years old   (D) forty years old

3. Broadwick tested a new parachute for—
   (A) her father   (B) the Navy
   (C) the Army   (D) fun

4. You can tell that Broadwick was—
   (A) cautious   (B) afraid
   (C) embarrassed   (D) brave

5. The word "secured" in line six means—
   (A) measured   (B) given
   (C) attached   (D) trusted

Whittier, Alaska, is an unusual town for many reasons. It is a hundred miles from the nearest city, and it has no roads that *lead* to any cities or towns. The winds are too high for planes and boats, so the only way to enter or leave Whittier is by train. But the most unusual thing about Whittier is that most of the people who live there live in the same building!

The buildings in Whittier include a store, a fire station, a restaurant, a small apartment house, and a fourteen-story apartment building where most people live. The big apartment also is home for the police, post office, school, church, library, museum, two theaters, and business offices. Whatever the people want is almost always in their own house.

---

1. The best title is—
   (A) Alaska—A Cold State
   (B) Building Roads in Alaska
   (C) A Town That Lives Together
   (D) Traveling by Airplane

2. The big apartment building in Whittier is—
   (A) two stories high   (B) three stories high
   (C) ten stories high   (D) fourteen stories high

3. People enter and leave Whittier by—
   (A) plane   (B) train
   (C) boat   (D) dog sled

4. Whittier, Alaska, is not near—
   (A) water   (B) a train station
   (C) other cities   (D) land

5. The word "lead" in line two means—
   (A) more   (B) go
   (C) lose   (D) push

At the age of thirteen, she took flying lessons. When she was sixteen, she got her pilot's license. She went on to college, sure that she wanted to be an astronaut. Then she bought a sports car, and everything else was pushed aside. When she decided to become a race car driver, she vowed that someday she would drive a car in the Indy 500, the biggest race of all.

First, though, she would have to prove that a woman belonged in the Indy 500. Most of the drivers, all men, did not want to race with a woman. "Not good enough," they hooted. "Doesn't have the *nerve*," they hissed. The woman did not give up. Then in the 1978 Indy 500, she realized her dream. Janet Guthrie became the first woman to finish the Indy 500.

1. The best title is—
   (A) The Indy 500
   (B) Driving to the Top
   (C) Dreaming
   (D) Race Cars

2. Janet once wanted to be—
   (A) a doctor   (B) a TV reporter
   (C) a teacher   (D) an astronaut

3. The Indy 500 is—
   (A) a sports car   (B) an auto race
   (C) an airplane   (D) a TV show

4. The best word to describe Janet Guthrie is—
   (A) scared   (B) lucky
   (C) determined   (D) thoughtful

5. The word "nerve" in line nine means—
   (A) power   (B) courage
   (C) strength   (D) skill

UNIT 18

The town of Cuero, Texas, says that it is the "Turkey Capital of the World." The people who live in Worthington, Minnesota, think that their town is the "Turkey Capital of the World." To *settle* which town is to be called the turkey capital, every year there is a race called the Great Gobbler Gallop.

Each town picks one turkey. Then they have a turkey race to see which turkey is faster. The town with the winning turkey is the "Turkey Capital" for the year.

The people work hard to raise the best turkey, but they also have a lot of fun. After the race, they have picnics and games. Then they wait for the next year's race.

---

1. The best title is—
   (A) Cuero, Texas
   (B) A Turkey Race
   (C) Worthington, Minnesota
   (D) Eating Turkeys

2. The turkey race is called the—
   (A) Thanksgiving Contest   (B) Turkey Trot
   (C) Great Gobbler Gallop   (D) Turkey Derby

3. The story says that after the turkey race there are—
   (A) cooking contests   (B) movies
   (C) fights   (D) picnics

4. Both Cuero and Worthington probably have a lot of—
   (A) cows   (B) turkeys
   (C) sheep   (D) dogs

5. The word "settle" in line three means—
   (A) decide   (B) open
   (C) build   (D) forget

UNIT 19

At a time when most fathers teach their children to play peekaboo, Laszlo Polgar was teaching his daughters to play chess. His encouragement has paid off. All three of his daughters are world champions. His oldest daughter, Zsuzsa, was the first woman in history to earn the title Grand Master.

The Polgar sisters have had to compete both on and off the chessboard. Until 1988, women were not allowed to play against men in world-class matches, even if they were more qualified. Zsuzsa and her sisters, Judit and Zsofia, have worked to bring *equality* to the world of chess.

Move by move, the Polgar sisters are winning. They are champions of chess and of women's rights.

1. The best title is—
   (A) Let's Play Chess
   (B) My Dad Laszlo
   (C) The Chess-Playing Polgar Sisters
   (D) No Women Allowed

2. Laszlo Polgar taught his daughters to play—
   (A) peekaboo   (B) piano
   (C) cards   (D) chess

3. The first woman to earn the title Grand Master was—
   (A) Zsuzsa Polgar   (B) Judit Polgar
   (C) Zsofia Polgar   (D) Laszlo Polgar

4. You can tell that the Polgar sisters are—
   (A) beautiful   (B) competitive
   (C) bad-tempered   (D) snobby

5. The word "equality" in line nine means—
   (A) goodness   (B) perfection
   (C) politeness   (D) fairness

UNIT 20

Dragons exist in stories. You know them as the fire-breathing monsters that attack knights and other people. Did you know that dragons exist in real life too? These dragons don't spit fire, but they are big and unfriendly.

Weighing up to three hundred pounds and growing to twelve feet, Komodo dragons take their name from their home, Komodo Island, in the western Pacific Ocean. A pilot discovered them after making a forced landing there. Of course, no one believed his stories. But when a museum sent scientists to the island, they took pictures and even brought back a few dragons for *display*. If you are lucky enough to live near a zoo that has Komodo dragons, be sure to see them.

1. The best title is—
    (A) A Story Come True
    (B) Finding Animals
    (C) Real-life Dragons
    (D) A Plane Crash

2. Komodo Island lies in the—
    (A) Sea of Japan
    (C) Gulf of Mexico
    (B) Atlantic Ocean
    (D) Pacific Ocean

3. The Komodo dragons were discovered by—
    (A) a knight
    (C) a pilot
    (B) a museum
    (D) a scientist

4. The best word to describe a Komodo dragon is—
    (A) fire-breathing
    (C) playful
    (B) real
    (D) imaginary

5. The word "display" in line ten means—
    (A) fire
    (C) laughs
    (B) death
    (D) show

UNIT 21

It happened in the state of New Mexico. A cowhand, who was riding his horse, thought he saw smoke in the distance. He rode over to see. When he got there, he was surprised to find no smoke at all. What he had seen were hundreds of bats flying out of a hole in the ground!

When the cowhand *peered* down into the hole, he was even more surprised. Deep underground, where the bats had come from, were giant caves and beautifully colored rocks.

Today, thousands of people visit these caves each year. They are known as the Carlsbad Caverns.

---

1. The best title is—
   (A) The Bats of New Mexico
   (B) How Well Cowhands Rode Horses
   (C) Mining in New Mexico
   (D) Discovering the Carlsbad Caverns

2. Hundreds of bats were coming out of a—
   (A) tree   (B) hole
   (C) lake   (D) fire

3. The Carlsbad Caverns were discovered by—
   (A) a soldier   (B) an Indian
   (C) a cowhand   (D) a pilot

4. Today, the Carlsbad Caverns are—
   (A) unknown   (B) forgotten
   (C) popular   (D) ruined

5. The word "peered" in line six means—
   (A) looked   (B) slept
   (C) played   (D) flew

UNIT 22

Are you bothered by mosquitoes in the summer? If you are, you should visit Griggsville, Illinois. This town has almost no mosquitoes in the summer, for a very strange reason.

Griggsville is called the "Purple Martin Capital of the World." Purple martins are birds that love to eat mosquitoes and other insects. The people of Griggsville have built special birdhouses on tall poles all around their town so that the birds have a place to stay when they are not feeding on mosquitoes.

The people of Griggsville are nice to the purple martins. In return, the purple martins make sure that there are no mosquitoes to *pester* the people.

---

1. The best title is—
   (A) Bothered by Mosquitoes
   (B) How Purple Martins Help Griggsville
   (C) What Purple Martins Look Like
   (D) What Mosquitoes Eat

2. Griggsville is located in—
   (A) Illinois
   (C) Canada
   (B) New York
   (D) Mississippi

3. The special birdhouses are built—
   (A) of glass
   (C) on tall poles
   (B) on water
   (D) under the ground

4. The story suggests that the people and the birds—
   (A) get bitten
   (C) are enemies
   (B) are partners
   (D) want to leave town

5. The word "pester" in line ten means—
   (A) help
   (C) bother
   (B) sell
   (D) feed

Jan played the tuba in her school band. She also had a pet squirrel. That's how the trouble began. One day the squirrel crawled into Jan's tuba. It was afraid to come out. Worse, Jan had to march in a parade that very day. She tried everything to get her pet to come out of the horn. She shook the tuba. She played some notes softly. She tapped it.

When nothing worked, Jan's father took Jan and the tuba with the squirrel in it to the veterinarian, a doctor who helps animals. The vet had an *inspiration*. He held five plump walnuts near the horn. In a few moments the squirrel crawled out of the tuba, looking for the walnuts. Jan marched in the parade with her pet tucked into its favorite spot, her pocket.

---

1. The best title is—
   (A) Squirrel in a Tuba
   (B) The Tuba Player
   (C) Walnuts
   (D) The Friendly Vet

2. Jan's squirrel liked best to stay in—
   (A) the tuba   (B) Jan's pocket
   (C) a cage   (D) a box

3. A veterinarian is—
   (A) a tuba player   (B) a band leader
   (C) a teacher   (D) an animal doctor

4. You can tell that Jan—
   (A) was angry   (B) did not like the tuba
   (C) was worried   (D) was afraid of the vet

5. The word "inspiration" in line eight means—
   (A) medicine   (B) idea
   (C) memory   (D) pet

Laurence White is a big star, but few people know what he looks like. The next time you watch TV or read a magazine, notice the ads in which only the person's hands show. The hands may belong to Laurence White.

Mr. White has perfect hands—at least, perfect in a way that photographers *approve*. They are not too big, and the skin is very smooth.

Is being a hand model easy? You judge. Try to hold your hands still for 30 minutes without moving a finger! Of course, you must be careful with your hands. That means no sports and no rough work. But all this is worth the trouble, Laurence says. "Being a hand model has made me a rich man—rich in the sense that I have a lot of free time."

1. The best title is—
   (A) Model Hands
   (B) TV Star
   (C) Laurence of TV
   (D) TV Model

2. One thing Laurence cannot do is—
   (A) play sports
   (B) cook
   (C) walk
   (D) drive a car

3. To photographers, perfect hands are—
   (A) heavy
   (B) skinny
   (C) strong
   (D) smooth

4. This story suggests that Laurence—
   (A) is out of work
   (B) enjoys the free time
   (C) plays the piano
   (D) plays sports

5. The word "approve" in line six means—
   (A) dislike
   (B) worry
   (C) like
   (D) change

A. Exercising Your Skill

Mosquitoes are one kind of animal most people could do without. They are tiny, yet they give a nasty bite. Mosquitoes are not the only little creatures that most people find it hard to like. Read this passage about another little animal that is not very popular. As you read, notice the underlined words.

> Vampires, as you may know, are the <u>villains</u> of many horror movies. These evil creatures go around <u>extracting</u> blood from sleeping people. Of course, human vampires are not real. They are found only in storybooks and movies. There is a real-life vampire, though. It is a kind of bat.
>
> <u>Contrary</u> to popular belief, the vampire bat is not a gigantic animal that <u>slaughters</u> animals or people by sucking all their blood. In fact, the vampire bat is a <u>miniature</u> creature, only about three inches long. True, the vampire bat does <u>exist</u> on blood. But it does not <u>consume</u> much. Here is how it gets its nightly <u>ration</u>. It <u>alights</u> quietly on the back of a sleeping animal, such as a cow. With its flat front teeth, it scrapes a bit of skin off the animal's back—just enough so a few drops of blood will begin to <u>ooze</u> out. Then it rolls its tongue into a tube-like shape and sucks up the blood. Most of the time the animal isn't even aware that it has provided the meal. It goes right on sleeping, while the tiny vampire bat <u>flutters</u> quietly off into the night.

Write each underlined word on your paper. Next to each word, write another word or phrase that means the same or almost the same thing.

B. Expanding Your Skill

Compare your list of words with those of your classmates. Why did you choose the words you did? Perhaps you looked at the *context*—the words and sentences around a word that give clues to its meaning. To your list, add some good context clues from your classmates' lists.

C. Exploring Language

Many words have more than one meaning. Read this sentence: Vampires are a *staple* part of many horror movies. The word *staple* in that sentence means "most important." A thin piece of bent wire that holds sheets of paper together is also called a *staple*, however.

Two meanings for each word are given below. Write two sentences for each word. Use a different meaning in each sentence.

1. **drop**: small amount of liquid
   make lower

2. **kind**: helpful and friendly
   group of things that are alike

3. **roll**: move up and down or side to side
   move on wheels

D. Expressing Yourself

Choose one of these activities.

1. Working with a classmate, put together a list of five more words that have more than one meaning. Make a poster of your word list. Include several meanings of each word and a sentence to show how each different meaning is used.

2. Words that are spelled alike but have different meanings are called *homographs*. The word *bear*, meaning "a kind of animal," and *bear*, meaning "to carry," are homographs. Some homographs sound alike; others do not.

   Words that sound alike but have different spellings and meanings are called *homophones*. The words *roll* and *role* are homophones.

   As a class project, draw up a list of as many homographs and homophones as you can think of. List them on separate charts.

One day in 1912, a farmer in West Virginia had a big surprise. He found large yellow fruit growing on a young apple tree. When he sent some of his strange apples to a nursery where apple trees were raised, people there offered to buy the tree for $5,000. The farmer agreed. Since the tree could not be moved, the nursery protected it with a high fence, for if it died, there might never be another tree like it anywhere in the world.

Although $5,000 may seem a high price for one apple tree, the nursery knew that they could raise many other trees from it by cutting off branches and *grafting* them to the root of a strong young tree. And that is just what they did. Thanks to that first tree, we now enjoy Golden Delicious apples today.

---

1. The best title is—
   (A) Apples
   (B) Growing Fruit
   (C) The $5,000 Tree
   (D) Red or Yellow?

2. The nursery protected the tree by—
   (A) grafting it   (B) moving it
   (C) fencing it in   (D) cutting it down

3. The tree grew—
   (A) white apples   (B) in two years
   (C) in a nursery   (D) in West Virginia

4. The story suggests that yellow apples were—
   (A) rare   (B) common
   (C) sour   (D) impossible

5. The word "grafting" in line ten means—
   (A) flying   (B) attaching
   (C) feeding   (D) moving

Jack Wurm was walking along the shore when he saw a bottle on the sand. As he *stooped* to pick it up, Jack saw a note inside. He couldn't believe what he read. Jack had found a note worth over six million dollars!

The note in the bottle was a will written by a very rich man who had since died. It said that whoever found the bottle would get half of his fortune. The bottle had been floating in the ocean for twelve years before Jack found it.

Jack Wurm didn't always pick up bottles at the shore, but you can be sure that he does now!

---

1. The best title is—
   (A) Walking at the Shore
   (B) Finding a Valuable Bottle
   (C) A Short Trip
   (D) Different Kinds of Bottles

2. Jack found the bottle—
   (A) in his house   (B) in a store
   (C) at the shore   (D) at a dump

3. The bottle had been floating in the ocean for—
   (A) 6 months   (B) 12 years
   (C) 6 years   (D) 12 months

4. The story suggests that the man who died—
   (A) lived in America   (B) died a poor man
   (C) had done an unusual thing (D) knew Jack Wurm

5. The word "stooped" in line two means—
   (A) bent over   (B) walked under
   (C) stood up   (D) fell asleep

Mrs. Steel couldn't understand it! She had taken off her $4,500 necklace, put it on a table, and gone into the kitchen. When she returned, a few minutes later, it was gone. Mrs. Steel called the police. The police couldn't find the necklace and couldn't figure out how it had been stolen!

Two weeks later, Mrs. Steel saw her dog, Rover, *munching* the fuzz from the living-room rug. Mrs. Steel thought, "Maybe the necklace fell on the rug and Rover ate it!" Mrs. Steel and her husband took Rover to a hospital. The doctor took an x-ray of Rover and saw the necklace in the stomach. The doctor took it out with a special tool. The mystery of the lost necklace had been solved!

1. The best title is—
   (A) How Hospitals Help People
   (B) Calling the Police
   (C) Finding a Lost Necklace
   (D) Mrs. Steel's Living-room Rug

2. Mrs. Steel and her husband took Rover to a—
   (A) dog show   (B) movie
   (C) hospital   (D) park

3. The lost necklace was found in—
   (A) the living room   (B) Rover's stomach
   (C) Rover's mouth   (D) a police car

4. In the story, the police—
   (A) couldn't help   (B) found the necklace
   (C) never came   (D) caught a dog

5. The word "munching" in line six means—
   (A) laughing   (B) eating
   (C) drinking   (D) making

Some famous Americans have told stories about imaginary creatures they *claimed* were real. The inventor Benjamin Franklin told a tall tale about monster whales that liked to swim up a huge waterfall. Franklin said that the whales were chasing their favorite food, a kind of fish called cod.

The well-known painter James Audubon drew a picture of a fish he said grew to be ten feet long. He named the four-hundred-pound monster Devil-Jack Diamond. Audubon said that the fish had hard diamond-shaped scales that not even a sharp weapon could go through. A person from France who believed Audubon's story published a book that described the monster fish. Who knows how many others believed Audubon's fish story?

1. The best title is—
   (A) Devil-Jack Diamond
   (B) Two Big Fish Found in France
   (C) Audubon's Paintings of Monster Fish
   (D) Franklin's and Audubon's Monsters

2. Devil-Jack Diamond was a—
   (A) whale
   (B) make-believe fish
   (C) well-known person
   (D) cod

3. Franklin told a story about—
   (A) a ten-foot fish
   (B) James Audubon
   (C) a monster whale
   (D) a French person

4. The story suggests that not all stories are—
   (A) famous
   (B) true
   (C) long
   (D) interesting

5. The word "claimed" in line two means—
   (A) said as fact
   (B) asked
   (C) discovered
   (D) said never

Do you think that the number thirteen is unlucky? If you do, maybe you should throw away any one-dollar bills that you have.

The American one-dollar bill has many thirteens on it. A *glance* at the back of the bill shows a pyramid with thirteen steps, and above the pyramid are two Latin words with thirteen letters. There is also an eagle that has thirteen arrows in one claw and a branch with thirteen leaves in the other claw. The eagle's shield has thirteen stripes, and there are thirteen stars over the bird's head.

If you know people who think that the number thirteen is unlucky—why not ask them for their one-dollar bills?

---

1. The best title is—
    (A) Latin Words on the One-dollar Bill
    (B) How to Make Money
    (C) One-dollar Bills and the Number Thirteen
    (D) The American Flag

2. The eagle has thirteen arrows in its—
    (A) tail   (B) beak
    (C) pocket   (D) claw

3. The two Latin words are—
    (A) below the eagle   (B) above the pyramid
    (C) next to the claw   (D) on the branch

4. If you know people who think thirteen is unlucky, you may become—
    (A) poorer   (B) richer
    (C) unlucky   (D) lonely

5. The word "glance" in line three means—
    (A) look   (B) sound
    (C) touch   (D) sniff

Who doesn't like pancakes? Many people in America eat them for breakfast with syrup. Americans are not the only ones who eat pancakes, though. In fact, no matter where you go in the world, you will find people eating them.

Pancakes have many different names. In Australia they are called "pikelets"; in Mexico, "tortillas." In France people *relish* very thin pancakes called "crepes." Ask for a pancake in Russia and you may get a "pannock," big enough to cover your plate, or you may get "sirnike," which are bite-sized. Filled with meat and a vegetable, any kind of pancake makes a main meal.

1. The best title is—
   (A) Eating
   (B) World Foods
   (C) Pancakes Across the World
   (D) Eating Around the World

2. The pancakes called "sirnike" can be found in—
   (A) Australia   (B) Russia
   (C) Israel   (D) France

3. One country the story does *not* mention is—
   (A) Australia   (B) Mexico
   (C) France   (D) Italy

4. Having read the story, you can say that pancakes are—
   (A) hard to make   (B) good for you
   (C) popular   (D) the same everywhere

5. The word "relish" in line six means—
   (A) like   (B) freeze
   (C) refuse   (D) boil

Have you ever ridden through a tunnel in a car? Some tunnels are very long. The longest tunnel in the world is 105 miles long, but no one has ever ridden through it. This tunnel is used to carry water!

Millions of people live in New York City, and they need a lot of water. They need it to drink and for other *purposes*. The nearest place where there is a great deal of fresh water is in the Catskill Mountains in upstate New York. So a tunnel was built to bring it to New York City. The tunnel took almost eight years to build.

Would you like to ride through this tunnel if there weren't any water in it?

---

1. The best title is—
   (A) The Shortest Tunnel in the World
   (B) How to Drive Through a Tunnel
   (C) The Longest Tunnel in the World
   (D) New York City

2. The story says that New York City needs a lot of—
   (A) tunnels   (B) water
   (C) food   (D) rain

3. The tunnel in the story is—
   (A) 13 miles long   (B) 8 miles long
   (C) 105 miles long   (D) 85 miles long

4. To the people in New York City, this tunnel is—
   (A) short   (B) valuable
   (C) useless   (D) cheap

5. The word "purposes" in line five means—
   (A) pictures   (B) games
   (C) uses   (D) times

Mary Patten was just sixteen years old in 1853 when she was married. Her husband was captain of a huge clipper ship, *Neptune's Car.* Three years later, Mary Patten was on board when the ship set sail from New York, bound for San Francisco. During the trip, Captain Patten became very sick. Rather than *entrust* the ship to the officers, Mary Patten took over herself. The crew did not like it, but Mary Patten was firm. She would be captain of *Neptune's Car* and care for her husband at the same time. Going without sleep for days at a time, Mary Patten guided the ship through terrible storms. Fifty days later she brought *Neptune's Car* safely into San Francisco harbor—a fine victory over the sea.

1. The best title is—
   (A) Mary Patten's Victory
   (B) Mary Patten's Crew
   (C) Sailing
   (D) Clipper Ships of 1853

2. *Neptune's Car* was sailing to—
   (A) New York   (B) Boston
   (C) San Francisco   (D) China

3. Mary took over as captain when she was—
   (A) sixteen years old   (B) fifty years old
   (C) not married   (D) married three years

4. The best word to describe Mary is—
   (A) foolish   (B) afraid
   (C) brave   (D) humble

5. The word "entrust" in line five means—
   (A) turn over   (B) sink
   (C) leave behind (D) lose

Many people today use an alarm to wake up in the morning. Years ago, before alarm clocks were invented, some people had strange ways of waking up.

One person had a bed that began to shake at a certain time. Another had a bed that would fall down when it was time to *arise*. A farmer trained a horse to kick his door every morning. A woman once even trained a bird to wake her up. The bird would fly to the woman's pillow and squawk, "Time to get up, you lazy thing."

Aren't you glad that we have alarm clocks today?

---

1. The best title is—
   (A) How Alarm Clocks Were Invented
   (B) A Trick Horse
   (C) Unusual Ways to Wake Up
   (D) Two Strange Beds

2. To wake up, the farmer in the story used a—
   (A) special bed   (B) cow
   (C) clock   (D) horse

3. The bird in the story would fly to the woman's—
   (A) table   (B) window
   (C) pillow   (D) chair

4. One thing that the story mentions is a—
   (A) blind man   (B) talking animal
   (C) grandfather   (D) sleeping fish

5. The word "arise" in line five means—
   (A) go to sleep   (B) rest
   (C) get up   (D) eat

It was Sunday, and Sherrill Conner thought that she would go for a *spin* in her boat. It was lucky for people in another boat that she did, because Sherrill saved their lives!

Sherrill was riding in her seventeen-foot boat when she heard calls for help. She raced toward the calls and soon saw a sinking boat. There in the freezing water were four adults and two children. They had been in the cold water for fifteen minutes and were about to drown. Sherrill pulled them into her boat and gave them first aid.

For her quick action, Sherrill received a letter from the President of the United States and four awards for bravery.

1. The best title is—
   (A) The President of the United States
   (B) Swimming in the Ocean
   (C) Fun on a Sunday
   (D) A Girl to the Rescue

2. The story says that Sherrill helped the people by giving them—
   (A) safety lessons   (B) dry clothes
   (C) first aid   (D) food

3. Sherrill received four awards for—
   (A) bravery   (B) going fast
   (C) talent   (D) good marks

4. Sherrill Conner saved—
   (A) two people   (B) four people
   (C) six people   (D) eight people

5. The word "spin" in line two means—
   (A) web   (B) jump
   (C) toss   (D) ride

How old is "old"? A field mouse is old when it is only three. A garter snake is old when it is six, while a cat is old when it is twenty. When a lion is thirty years old, it is as old as a person of seventy. Compared to most animals, people live a very long time. Among animals, only some kinds of turtles live longer than humans.

"Old" means different ages for different kinds of plants, too. A marigold plant is old after only three or four months. Some trees, however, can *survive* for hundreds—even thousands—of years. Redwoods that grow along the coast of California are still young at 500, while bristlecone pines live for over four thousand years. The oldest living tree is a bristlecone pine named Methuselah, which is more than 4,600 years old.

---

1. The best title is—
   (A) Methuselah
   (B) What "Old" Means to Living Things
   (C) The World's Oldest Things
   (D) The Ages of Animals and People

2. A cat is thought to be old at—
   (A) six   (B) twenty
   (C) ten   (D) twelve

3. The oldest trees are found in—
   (A) New Jersey   (B) Canada
   (C) California   (D) Europe

4. Compared with a bristlecone pine, an old redwood is—
   (A) old   (B) the same age
   (C) young   (D) wider

5. The word "survive" in line eight means—
   (A) lose branches   (B) be sick
   (C) live   (D) die

Many countries have sports in which their own people do very well. The United States has *excellent* football players, and in Canada hockey is the national sport. China has a sport at which the Chinese are the best in the world—table tennis. Table tennis is played like tennis but on a table. It is also called Ping-Pong.

In China, over one million people play table tennis regularly. The equipment does not cost much, so almost anyone can afford it. The Chinese have teams that travel all around the world. They usually beat everyone.

It might surprise you to find out that while table tennis is a very popular sport in China, so is basketball!

---

1. The best title is—
   (A) Eating in America
   (B) Another Name for Table Tennis
   (C) Table Tennis in China
   (D) Hockey—A National Sport

2. Another popular sport in China is—
   (A) soccer   (B) boxing
   (C) basketball   (D) hockey

3. A country that has excellent football players is—
   (A) the United States   (B) France
   (C) Canada   (D) Mexico

4. The story does *not* mention a sport played in—
   (A) the United States   (B) Canada
   (C) Russia   (D) China

5. The word "excellent" in line two means—
   (A) very young   (B) poor
   (C) small   (D) very good

Do you like to blow a whistle? Most people do. Railroad engineers even get paid to blow a whistle. It's part of their job, because every whistle has a different meaning.

A *number of* short toots is a warning to people or animals on the track. A long whistle means that the train is nearing a station or railroad crossing. Three short toots mean that the train is going to back up or stop at the next station.

The next time you hear a train whistle, be sure to listen. See if you can tell what it means.

---

1. The best title is—
   (A) Learning to Ride
   (B) What Train Whistles Mean
   (C) Why Trains Stop at Stations
   (D) A Railroad Engineer's Job

2. A long whistle may mean that the train is—
   (A) empty   (B) backing up
   (C) nearing a station   (D) near an animal

3. The story says that every whistle has—
   (A) no meaning   (B) a different meaning
   (C) the same meaning   (D) a soft sound

4. To know the meaning of a train whistle, you must be able to—
   (A) read   (B) write
   (C) count   (D) run

5. The words "a number of" in line four mean—
   (A) one   (B) several
   (C) millions of   (D) no

Most of us learn what the weather will be from reading a newspaper or watching TV. Often we can learn as much from watching animals. If you see ants building huge mounds around their homes, you can expect rain. The mounds act like dams to keep water out of the ants' underground homes. If more bees are flying around your yard than is normal, keep an eye on them. Rain will follow about two hours after they disappear into their hives. You can also look under the leaves on trees for butterflies. This is where they like to hide just before a storm. They must protect their *fragile* wings. Watching insects for signs of rain can be fun. Who knows? You may even forecast the weather better than the scientists!

1. The best title is—
    (A) Rain and the Insects
    (B) Weather
    (C) Animals
    (D) Nature's Cold Weather Signs

2. Just before a big rainstorm, ants will—
    (A) eat often   (B) weave their webs
    (C) hide under leaves   (D) build huge mounds

3. An insect the story does *not* mention is the—
    (A) ant   (B) wasp
    (C) bee   (D) butterfly

4. Scientists must have studied these insects' signs—
    (A) never   (B) only in the fall
    (C) two times   (D) many times

5. The word "fragile" in line nine means—
    (A) strong   (B) delicate
    (C) natural   (D) tough

A. Exercising Your Skill

A good title sums up the main idea of a paragraph in just a few words. Read this paragraph and write a title for it. Then write two sentences from the paragraph that led you to think of your title.

Too much snow in one place can cause a lot of harm—to the land, to people, to buildings. In general, however, snow is quite helpful. A good covering of snow on a farmer's field helps keep tender plants alive. Air under the snow is warmer than air above it. To prove how much warmer it can be, try this test. Look for a good-sized snowdrift—five feet high is the best. Using a thermometer, take the temperature at the top of the snow pile. Then plunge the thermometer deep into the drift—all the way to the ground, if you can reach it. Wait a few minutes, then pull the thermometer out. When you read it this time, you may be surprised how much warmer the temperature is.

B. Expanding Your Skill

Usually a paragraph will have a main idea sentence. It may not always be the first sentence in the paragraph. Sometimes it will be the last sentence, or it may appear somewhere in the middle of the paragraph. Find the main idea sentence in this paragraph. Write the sentence on your paper.

A quick thaw caused by a sudden rise in the temperature may cause a snow slide in the mountains. A quick thaw followed by a freeze, or a heavy fall of snow on an already deep layer, may also bring on snow slides. If any of these conditions exist, watch out! Snow on mountain slopes can be extremely dangerous. Many people have been killed or injured by a large mass of snow sliding down quickly.

C. Exploring Language

Write a paragraph of five or six sentences using one of the following main idea sentences at the beginning. After you have written the paragraph, give it a title (two to five words) that sums up the main idea.

1. When it comes to the weather, there is one thing you can always be sure of—it will change.
2. Weather plays an important role in what we do and when we do it.
3. Because of the jobs they hold, some people must know what the weather will be like.
4. Everything looks different after a snowfall.
5. Here are some safety rules to follow if you are caught in a bad storm.

D. Expressing Yourself

Choose one of these activities.

1. Find information about bad storms such as hurricanes and blizzards. Prepare a report on your findings.

2. Give a short talk to your classmates in which you tell about the scariest storm you have been through.

3. Locate some poems that tell about snow or other weather conditions. Read a few of the ones you like best to your classmates.

4. Try to imagine what it would be like to be caught in the middle of the ocean in a small boat during a big storm. Write a description of what is going on around you, how you feel about it, and what you will do if you reach land safely.

Many people who have lived in big cities and small towns think that people walk faster in the cities. They always seem to be in a hurry. A group of scientists decided to find out if city people really do walk faster.

The scientists went to many big cities and small towns. They timed how fast the people walked. The scientists found out that city walkers move at almost twice the *rate* of walkers in small towns.

Why do people in the cities walk faster? Maybe it's because they are more nervous. Maybe it's because they have more places to go. What do you think is the reason?

___

1. The best title is—
   (A) How Fast Scientists Walk
   (B) Walking in Cities and Small Towns
   (C) Walking to Get Someplace
   (D) A Good Way to Travel

2. Walking in the city and the country was timed by—
   (A) scientists   (B) teachers
   (C) race drivers   (D) the police

3. People in cities walk—
   (A) more slowly   (B) later
   (C) easily   (D) faster

4. If country walkers move about 2 miles per hour, city walkers move about—
   (A) 1 mile per hour   (B) 2 miles per hour
   (C) 4 miles per hour   (D) 10 miles per hour

5. The word "rate" in line seven means—
   (A) study   (B) speed
   (C) return   (D) race

Most people are happy to have one dog or maybe two. But not Susan Butcher. She owns 150 dogs, all Alaskan huskies. Susan is one of the best sled dog racers in the world. She got that title when she won her third Iditarod sled dog race. ("Iditarod" is an Indian name meaning "distant place.") The race across Alaska is held every March. The course runs 1,152 miles from Anchorage to Nome. Along the way the racers and their dogs cross two mountain ranges, frozen rivers, part of an ocean, and a burned-out forest.

The winner was *awarded* $50,000. But money is not why Susan races. "I never got into this to win a lot of money," she says, "but to live just the way I want, to do what I love to do."

1. The best title is—
   (A) What "Iditarod" Means
   (B) Sled Dog Champ
   (C) Sled Dogs
   (D) Alaskan Weather

2. The Iditarod race is run from—
   (A) Nome to Anchorage   (B) Nome to Alaska
   (C) Anchorage to Nome   (D) Alaska to Anchorage

3. The word "Iditarod" means—
   (A) Alaska   (B) dogsled
   (C) distant place   (D) husky

4. To win the Iditarod, a person must be—
   (A) tall   (B) strong
   (C) afraid of dogs   (D) afraid of heights

5. The word "awarded" in line nine means—
   (A) taken   (B) shown
   (C) given   (D) forgotten

Did you ever wonder which animal is the biggest? There are really two answers to that question.

The "heaviest" animal is the blue whale. Today there are still some swimming in the ocean. The heaviest one ever seen *probably* weighed about two hundred tons—heavier than the dinosaurs of long ago. That's thirty-five times as heavy as an African elephant or about as heavy as a hundred big automobiles.

The "tallest" animal is the giraffe, which is found in certain areas of Africa. The tallest giraffe ever known stood nineteen feet tall—from the top of its head to the ground. That's three times as tall as a tall person.

---

1. The best title is—
   (A) The Tall Giraffe
   (B) The Blue Whale
   (C) The Biggest Animals
   (D) Heavier than Dinosaurs

2. The tallest animal is the—
   (A) reindeer   (B) giraffe
   (C) elephant   (D) moose

3. The heaviest animal is the—
   (A) hippo   (B) elephant
   (C) blue whale   (D) giraffe

4. The story does *not* mention—
   (A) giraffes   (B) blue whales
   (C) tigers   (D) dinosaurs

5. The word "probably" in line four means—
   (A) cannot have   (B) never
   (C) most likely   (D) as a baby

Most children walk to school. Others ride in a car or on the school bus. Some children even ride bicycles. But the children who live on the island of Ou in the Pacific Ocean don't do any of these—they use stilts. Stilts are long poles. People who walk with stilts are carried high above the ground.

The children who live on Ou have to go to a school which is on a *nearby* island. The water between the islands is not deep enough to use a boat so the pupils walk on stilts. Each day they walk across the 1,400 feet of water on their ten-foot-high stilts. Their teacher can easily tell if they fell on the way to school.

1. The best title is—
   (A) What the Children of Ou Learn in School
   (B) Riding a School Bus
   (C) How to Make Stilts
   (D) A Strange Way to Go to School

2. The island of Ou is in the—
   (A) Red Sea   (B) Indian Ocean
   (C) China Sea   (D) Pacific Ocean

3. The children of Ou walk to school on—
   (A) large rocks   (B) five-foot stilts
   (C) ten-foot stilts   (D) a long bridge

4. The teacher can tell if the children fell because they would be—
   (A) bleeding   (B) dry
   (C) wet   (D) singing

5. The word "nearby" in line seven means—
   (A) always   (B) close
   (C) open   (D) never

Perhaps you have heard the saying "as slow as cold molasses." Well, molasses may be slow to pour because it is a thick syrup. But once it gets moving, it can cause a whole lot of *damage*. On January 15, 1919, a tank holding one and a half million gallons of molasses blew up in Boston. A wave of molasses, forty feet high, flowed down the city streets. Even the cold winter weather did not stop it. The wave knocked down houses and part of an overhead railway, then sank a ship in the harbor. Before it gave out, eleven people had been killed and at least fifty more were hurt. It took weeks to clean up the mess. Today a playground sits where the great molasses tank once stood. And on very hot summer nights, people say you can still smell molasses!

---

1. The best title is—
   (A) Seeing Boston in January
   (B) A Boston Winter
   (C) The Great Molasses Flood
   (D) How Molasses is made

2. The molasses started to flow when a—
   (A) storm came up   (B) ship sank
   (C) tank blew up   (D) worker opened a tank

3. The event took place in—
   (A) Rhode Island   (B) New York
   (C) Chicago   (D) Boston

4. A flowing wall of molasses is—
   (A) very sweet   (B) dangerous
   (C) easy to stop   (D) fun to watch

5. The word "damage" in line three means—
   (A) harm   (B) traffic
   (C) pleasure   (D) rain

Crabb, Texas, a small town south of Houston, is so small that for years it did not have a mayor. A few years ago, the people of Crabb decided they would choose a mayor. Three people ran for the honor. Two were retired people, and the third was a thirteen-year-old boy. When the votes were counted, Brian Zimmerman was declared the winner. That made him the youngest mayor in the United States.

Being *elected* mayor did not mean that Brian could serve, however. You must be eighteen years old to hold public office in Texas. Brian didn't seem to mind. He was happy just knowing that most of the 225 people in Crabb voted for him. Besides, a movie was made about the boy\mayor of Crabb, Texas.

1. The best title is—
   (A) Crabb, Texas
   (B) Boy Mayor
   (C) Voting for Mayor
   (D) Texas Election

2. Crabb is near—
   (A) Texas
   (B) Houston
   (C) Dallas
   (D) Fort Worth

3. Crabb has—
   (A) 2,225 people
   (B) 225 people
   (C) two hundred people
   (D) two thousand people

4. To Brian Zimmerman, winning the most votes was—
   (A) impossible
   (B) hard to do
   (C) an accident
   (D) an honor

5. The word "elected" in line seven means—
   (A) chosen
   (B) arrested
   (C) passed over for
   (D) missed as

Would you like to have some fun? Throw a bottle away. If you live near water, it's easy. Simply write a note with your name and address and put it in a bottle. Ask whoever finds the bottle to write back to you. It will be interesting to see how far the bottle travels and fun to get a letter from someone you have never met.

A person who lived in Ohio *heaved* a bottle with a note into the Mississippi River. Soon it was forgotten about. But five years later a letter arrived. Someone had found the bottle in Scotland—6,800 miles away.

Why don't you throw a bottle away? It may be fun!

1. The best title is—
   (A) The Ohio River
   (B) Fun with Bottles
   (C) How to Write a Letter
   (D) Traveling Is Fun

2. The bottle found in Scotland had traveled for—
   (A) five weeks   (B) two years
   (C) one hundred days   (D) five years

3. The bottle that traveled to Scotland started in—
   (A) Ohio   (B) Paris
   (C) England   (D) Oklahoma

4. The story suggests that bottles sometimes—
   (A) cost a lot   (B) travel slowly
   (C) are hard to get   (D) are very big

5. The word "heaved" in line six means—
   (A) broke   (B) swam
   (C) saved   (D) threw

Don't worry if your dog is getting old. There's a home for aging dogs that has opened near Egg Harbor, New Jersey.

"When dogs reach ten or twelve years of age, they have the same type of health problems as old people," says the owner of the Barkwood Kennels. "We make life a lot easier for them."

Rooms at the kennels are heated and air-conditioned. The baths are tiled. Doctors are *available* all the time. The dogs like it at their old-age home. At the Barkwood Kennels they say, "Old dogs need care, just as old people do. They care for us, and we should care for them."

1. The best title is—
    (A) An Old People's Home
    (B) The Health Problems of Old People
    (C) Doctors on Call
    (D) A Home for Old Dogs

2. The rooms at Barkwood Kennels are—
    (A) very small   (B) not nice
    (C) heated   (D) for old people

3. The home for old dogs is in—
    (A) New York   (B) Baltimore
    (C) England   (D) New Jersey

4. The story suggests that a dog is old at—
    (A) 5 years of age   (B) 7 years of age
    (C) 9 years of age   (D) 11 years of age

5. The word "available" in line seven means—
    (A) never there   (B) sick
    (C) ready to be used   (D) ahead

Five-year-old Levan Merritt loved to visit the zoo. On one visit he climbed onto a wall that separates people from gorillas. Levan lost his balance and fell twenty feet down into the gorilla pit. The fall knocked him out. Levan's parents were *petrified* with fear. They felt their son would be killed. Then Jambo, a 400-pound gorilla, came over and stood by Levan. Each time another ape tried to get at the boy, Jambo shoved it aside. "Jambo was just like a dad," Levan's mother said later. "He was lovely." Soon a zoo worker climbed the wall and carried Levan away. When he got better, Levan went back to the zoo. This time he stayed off the wall. But he talked to Jambo just the same. "I'm not scared," Levan said. "Jambo looked after me, didn't he? Jambo is my friend."

1. The best title is—
    (A) At the Zoo
    (B) Gorilla Rescue
    (C) Watching Gorillas
    (D) Jambo Falls from the Wall

2. Levan met Jambo when he—
    (A) went to a party
    (B) fell into the gorilla pit
    (C) was in school
    (D) was six years old

3. When Levan fell into the gorilla pit, he—
    (A) began to cry
    (B) played with Jambo
    (C) was knocked out
    (D) tried to climb back out

4. Jambo—
    (A) was a mean gorilla
    (B) hated the other apes
    (C) was afraid of Levan
    (D) knew Levan was in danger

5. The word "petrified" in line four means—
    (A) laughing
    (B) finished
    (C) aging
    (D) dazed

Most hotels look like hotels, but not the hotel built at New York's Coney Island in 1881. This hotel—believe it or not—looked like an elephant, and that's what it was called, the Elephant Hotel!

The Elephant Hotel was shaped just like an elephant. It had tusks that were thirty-six feet long. It was seven stories high, and its metal skin had windows that *overlooked* the sea. Inside, there were a hall eighty feet long and thirty-four rooms for guests. The eyes of the Elephant Hotel were windows four feet wide, which could be seen for miles.

What a strange sight for ships that passed in the distance!

1. The best title is—
   (A) The Elephant Hotel
   (B) Tusks Thirty-six Feet Long
   (C) New York's Coney Island
   (D) Hotels That Look like Hotels

2. The Elephant Hotel was—
   (A) like most hotels   (B) five stories high
   (C) seven stories high   (D) ninety feet long

3. The story says that part of the hotel was made of—
   (A) wood   (B) metal
   (C) plastic   (D) cloth

4. People seeing the Elephant Hotel for the first time must have been—
   (A) unhappy   (B) tired
   (C) surprised   (D) bored

5. The word "overlooked" in line six means—
   (A) looked out on   (B) fished
   (C) easily shut   (D) loved

Watch out for that bee! Although it may look like a regular honey-bee, it may be an insect new to the United States—a killer bee! This new kind of bee first appeared in Brazil in the late 1950s. Brought from Africa as part of an experiment, some bees escaped. When these bees mated with regular honeybees, killer bees were born. Since then, these bees have spread throughout much of South America, Central America, and Mexico. They *reached* Texas in 1990.

The name "killer bee" is confusing, though. The sting of one killer bee is not worse than the sting of a regular honeybee. But killer bees are fighters. If they are bothered, they are likely to attack in a group. Then they are very dangerous. Scientists hope to stop these bees.

1. The best title is—
   (A) The Story of Bees
   (B) Beware of the Bees
   (C) How Bees Make Honey
   (D) Bees from the United States

2. Bees were brought from Africa—
   (A) to kill other bees   (B) for an experiment
   (C) to help Africans   (D) to make honey

3. "Killer bees" got their name because they are—
   (A) shy   (B) confusing
   (C) fighters   (D) hard workers

4. The creation of "killer bees" was—
   (A) not planned   (B) planned
   (C) unknown   (D) necessary

5. The word "reached" in line seven means—
   (A) feared   (B) left
   (C) arrived in   (D) died in

Do you know that one part of a plant may be eaten while another part of the same plant may make you sick or even kill you? This is true.

People can eat cherries, but the twig of the cherry tree is poisonous. Peaches are good for people, but the leaves are *risky* to eat. So are the leaves and stems of tomato and potato plants. Perhaps the most dangerous is rhubarb. While the stalk is tasty and good for the health, the leaves have even killed people.

The best rule to follow is this: Unless you know it is safe, never eat any plant.

1. The best title is—
   (A) Planting Potatoes
   (B) Plants Can Be Dangerous
   (C) Peaches, Pears, and Plums
   (D) Friendly Plants

2. The part of the cherry tree that is not good is the—
   (A) cherry   (B) root
   (C) twig   (D) leaf

3. The part of the peach tree that is not good is the—
   (A) bark   (B) leaves
   (C) peach   (D) root

4. You can tell that—
   (A) all plants are good to eat   (B) parts of some plants are dangerous
   (C) no plants are good to eat   (D) people should eat everything

5. The word "risky" in line five means—
   (A) sweet   (B) safe
   (C) dangerous   (D) salty

A. Exercising Your Skill

Susan Butcher was *determined*. Levan Merritt was *unafraid*. The stories you read in Unit 40 and Unit 47 did not use these words in describing those people, but you can guess that the words are accurate from clues in their stories. Butcher raced sled dogs more than one thousand miles across frozen Alaska. Merritt, not realizing the danger, climbed onto a wall that separated people from gorillas. Those are clues that lead us to call Butcher determined and Merritt unafraid.

When you use clues to figure out something the author doesn't say directly, you are making an **inference**. Read this story to see what inference you can make about Laura.

> Laura watched sadly as her friends chased one another up and down the rink. They had been playing a game of tag on ice for the last hour. Laura had always been the fastest skater in her group. No one was ever able to tag her, but sometimes she took great risks in order to avoid being tagged. Her mother often warned her to be more careful when she skated. "I guess I should have listened to her," Laura said to herself.

Read the three sentences below. Which is an inference you can make from clues in the story?

1. Laura was too tired to play tag on ice.
2. Laura had hurt herself skating.
3. Laura did not want to play tag on ice.

On your paper, write two clues from the story that led to the inference you made. Then discuss your inference with your classmates. Did you all agree? What clues did others use to make an inference?

B. Expanding Your Skill

Working in groups, rewrite the story of Laura and the game of tag on ice. This time include clues that will show that Laura did not like to skate. Remember, you don't want to come right out and say she didn't like skating. You will want readers to infer, or guess, this from the words you use.

C. Exploring Language

An inference is not a wild guess. Inferences are always based upon clues. For example, suppose you read that a woman was packing a suitcase and putting papers into her briefcase. You might infer that she is getting ready for a business trip. You could not infer, though, that she *wants* to be going on the trip. There are no clues to tell you that.

On your paper, write an inference that you can make based on these happenings.

1. Terry tossed her school books on her bed and reached into the closet for her tennis racket.

   _____

2. Sam took a quick look at his watch, then dashed down the hall to Room 25.

   _____

3. The moment the football game appeared on TV, Sherry turned the set off.

   _____

4. Toby's mother looked at his report card and groaned.

   _____

5. Rosa's dog saw her fill up the bathtub and ran to hide under the bed.

   _____

D. Expressing Yourself

Choose one of these activities.

1. Think up two more scenes like the ones in Part C. Describe each scene in words or draw a picture of it. What inferences can your classmates make based on your words or pictures?

2. Working with two or three of your classmates, act out one of the fables of Aesop. See if those who are watching and listening can guess the moral of the fable.